YOU'RE INVITED TO A
MOTH BALL

A Nighttime Insect Celebration

YOU'RE INVITED TO A
MOTH BALL

A Nighttime Insect Celebration

AUTHOR: Loree Griffin Burns

PHOTOGRAPHER: Ellen Harasimowicz

WHERE: Your backyard

WHEN: Right now!

Turn the page to RSVP!

Charlesbridge

To Charlotte, Harker, Shivani, Lily, Eamon, Leah,
Chloe, and Arrow, who accepted our invitation—L.G.B.

To Becky, Iliana, and Haley, with love—E.H.

Special thanks to Dr. David Horn, formerly of Ohio State University and Ohio
Biological Survey; Teá Kesting-Handly, curator of www.sphingidae.us, an in-depth study
of sphinx moths in the United States; and Dr. Jennifer Forman Orth, environmental
biologist at the Massachusetts Department of Agricultural Resources.

Please note: The moths in this book are not always pictured to scale.

At the time of publication, all URLs printed in this book were accurate and active. Charlesbridge,
the author, and the photographer are not responsible for the content or accessibility of any website.

Published by Charlesbridge
85 Main Street, Watertown, MA 02472
(617) 926-0329 • www.charlesbridge.com

Library of Congress Cataloging-in-Publication Data
Names: Burns, Loree Griffin, author. | Harasimowicz, Ellen, photographer.
Title: You're invited to a moth ball: a nighttime insect celebration /
    Loree Griffin Burns; photographs by Ellen Harasimowicz.
Other titles: You are invited to a moth ball
Description: Watertown, MA: Charlesbridge, [2020]
Identifiers: LCCN 2019008030 (print) | LCCN 2019018377 (ebook) |
    ISBN 9781632898340 (ebook) | ISBN 9781632898357 (ebook pdf) |
    ISBN 9781580896863 (reinforced for library use: alk. paper)
Subjects: LCSH: Moths–Juvenile literature. | Moths–Behavior–Juvenile literature.
Classification: LCC QL544.2 (ebook) | LCC QL544.2 .B79275 2020 (print) |
        DDC   595.78–dc23
LC record available at https://lccn.loc.gov/2019008030

Printed in China
(hc) 10 9 8 7 6 5 4 3 2 1

Display type set in Liberty & Love by Creativeqube Design and Paquita Pro by Juanjo Lopez
Text type set in Berthold Baskerville by Adobe
Color separations by Colourscan Print Co Pte Ltd, Singapore
Printed by 1010 Printing International Limited in Huizhou, Guangdong, China
Production supervision by Brian G. Walker
Designed by Sarah Richards Taylor

What's that? You don't know what a moth ball is? Please come anyway! You can learn as we go.

A moth ball is a special kind of party. Instead of celebrating a birthday or marking a holiday, we're honoring a spectacular insect.

You know which insect, right?

feathery antennae

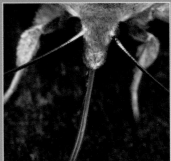

unfurled proboscis

You got it. The moth. There are more than 150,000 different moth species, and hundreds of them—possibly thousands—live where you do. A moth ball is a way to meet them. Up close.

chunky, hairy abdomen

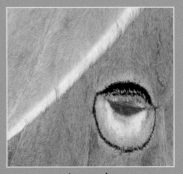

wing scales

We need flashlights, a notebook, a pencil, a camera, and tools for looking closely at moths. And to persuade moths to join us, we need a rope, a large light-colored sheet, some clothespins, and a special light bulb or two.

pencil

headlamp

camera

magnifying glass

notebook

flashlight

magnifying loupe

ruler

Did I mention we get to stay up late?
Because we do!

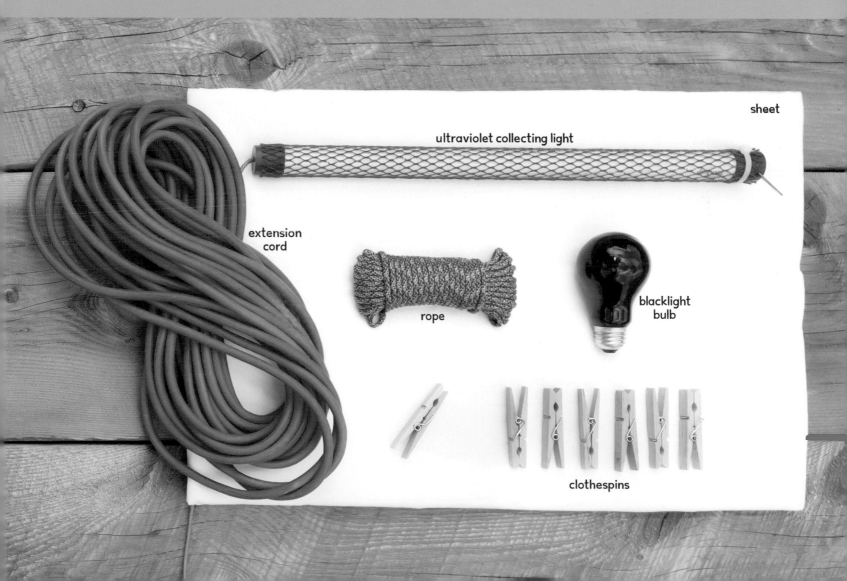

sheet

ultraviolet collecting light

extension
cord

rope

blacklight
bulb

clothespins

Before it gets dark, we set up our light station . . .

. . . and make a snack.

If rotting bananas and brown sugar aren't your favorite party foods, don't worry. These treats are for the moths! Grab a paintbrush, and we'll set the mixture out for them.

While we wait for the sun to set, let's study up on moths.

MOTHS AND LIGHTS

There are different kinds of light, some visible to our eyes and some not. Moths are drawn to all of them. Scientists don't really know why. What we do know is that the light we typically call ultraviolet is the kind most enticing to moths.

MOTHS AND BAIT

Some types of moths are less attracted to light than others. Luckily, these moths are often drawn to something else: nectar. They seek out the syrup produced by flowering plants (or the sap produced by trees). When they find it, they use their long mouthpart, or proboscis, to sip it. The sugary bait we mixed up is a homemade nectar. By painting it around the yard, we invite even more moths to the party.

MOTHS VERSUS BUTTERFLIES

How can you know for sure if you're looking at a moth or a butterfly? The time of day is one clue: most butterflies are active during the day and most moths at night. The best way to know which one you're looking at, though, is to study its antennae. Butterfly antennae are long and thin, and always have a thick knob, or club, at the end. Moth antennae are also long, sometimes pointed and sometimes feathery, but never clubbed.

IDENTIFYING MOTHS

The details of a moth's appearance and a good field guide can help you determine what species of moth you've found. Pay attention to a moth's overall size and shape, the way it holds its wings at rest (spread wide? over its body?), the presence or absence of hair on its body, and the marks on its wings (spots? stripes? zigzags?).

There are other clues, too. Different moth species live in different habitats. A moth's life cycle, particularly the caterpillar stage, depends on the plants available in its environment. So noting the habitat in which you found your moth (woodland? wetland? meadow?) and the types of plants and trees in that habitat can sometimes help you identify your moth.

Hey, is it dark outside yet?
Great. Let's go mothing!

What do we do now that the moths are here?
We have a ball, of course! Cavort. Observe.
Take notes and draw what you see. Be gentle.
Take some pictures if you like.

The number of moths might be small at first. Be patient. On a warm night, moths become more active as the night gets darker and the hour gets later.

Some people never, not once in their whole lives, connect with moths this way. So take your time. Soak it all in.

And don't forget to check the sugar bait. There might be more moths to meet.

Party on, friends! Be kind to your guests. Watch them sip homemade nectar, and marvel at how they do it.

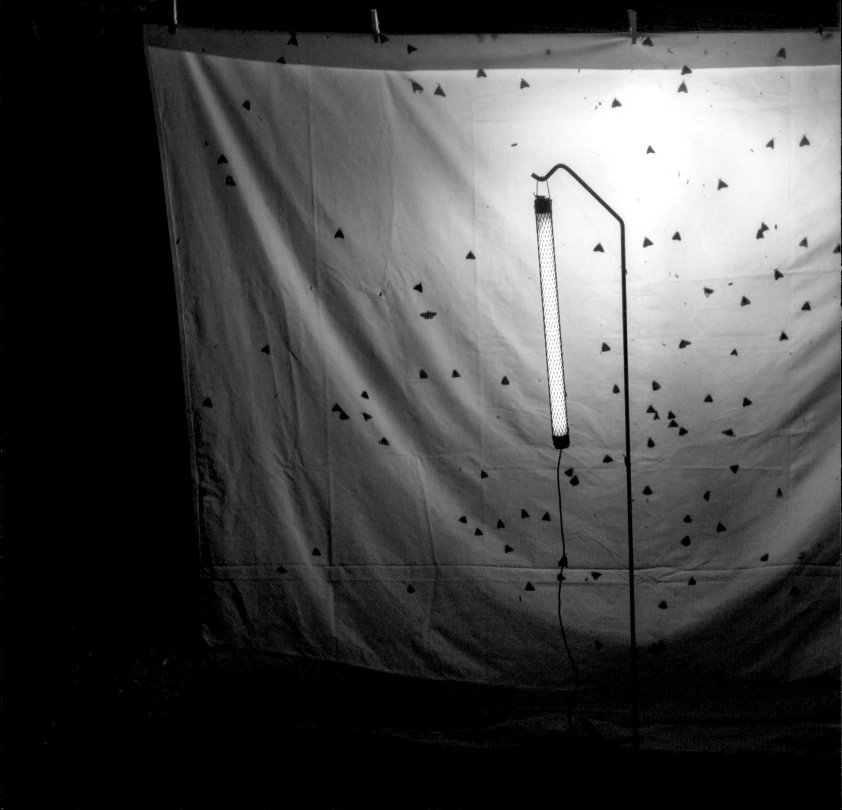

The time will come to end your party. Don't be sad. Some of the moths will hang around all night, even until morning, as long as the lights are on. When you've learned all you can, and you're ready to rest . . .

. . . whisper your thanks to all
the moths that stopped by tonight.

Wasn't that a ball?

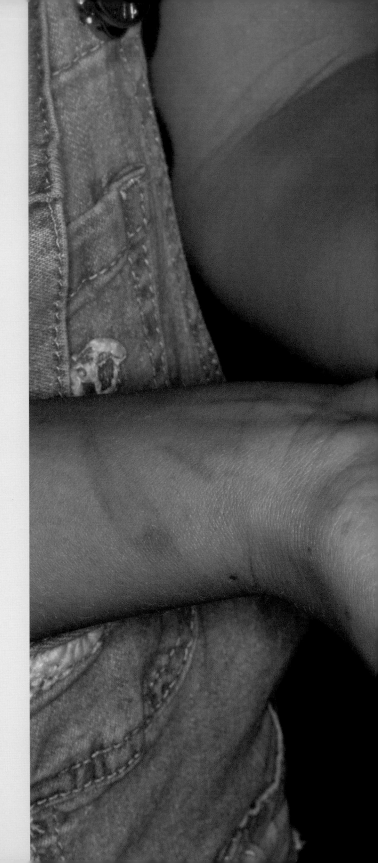

MORE ABOUT MOTH BALLS

Where Can I Go to a Moth Ball?

Moth-watching events are held at nature centers and other venues, especially during National Moth Week each July. If you can't find an event near you, host a moth ball of your own!

Why Participate in a Moth Ball?

Scientists estimate that there are 150,000 species of moths in the world. That's a huge treasury of insects we usually overlook just because we're sleeping when they're active. By inviting moths into your yard with lights or bait and by paying attention to the moths that visit, you'll be learning something important about the wildlife around you. And you can report what you learn, too! (Visit the Butterflies and Moths of North America and Discover Life websites listed on page 40 to find out how.)

THE LIFE CYCLE & PARTS OF A MOTH

Like many insects, moths have a four-part life cycle: egg, caterpillar, pupa, and adult. First there's an egg, and out of that egg hatches a caterpillar. After eating its way through several growth stages, or instars, the caterpillar finds a safe hiding place to become a pupa. (Some moth species build their own hiding place, called a cocoon.) During the inactive pupal life stage, a complete body transformation takes place. Then an adult moth emerges.

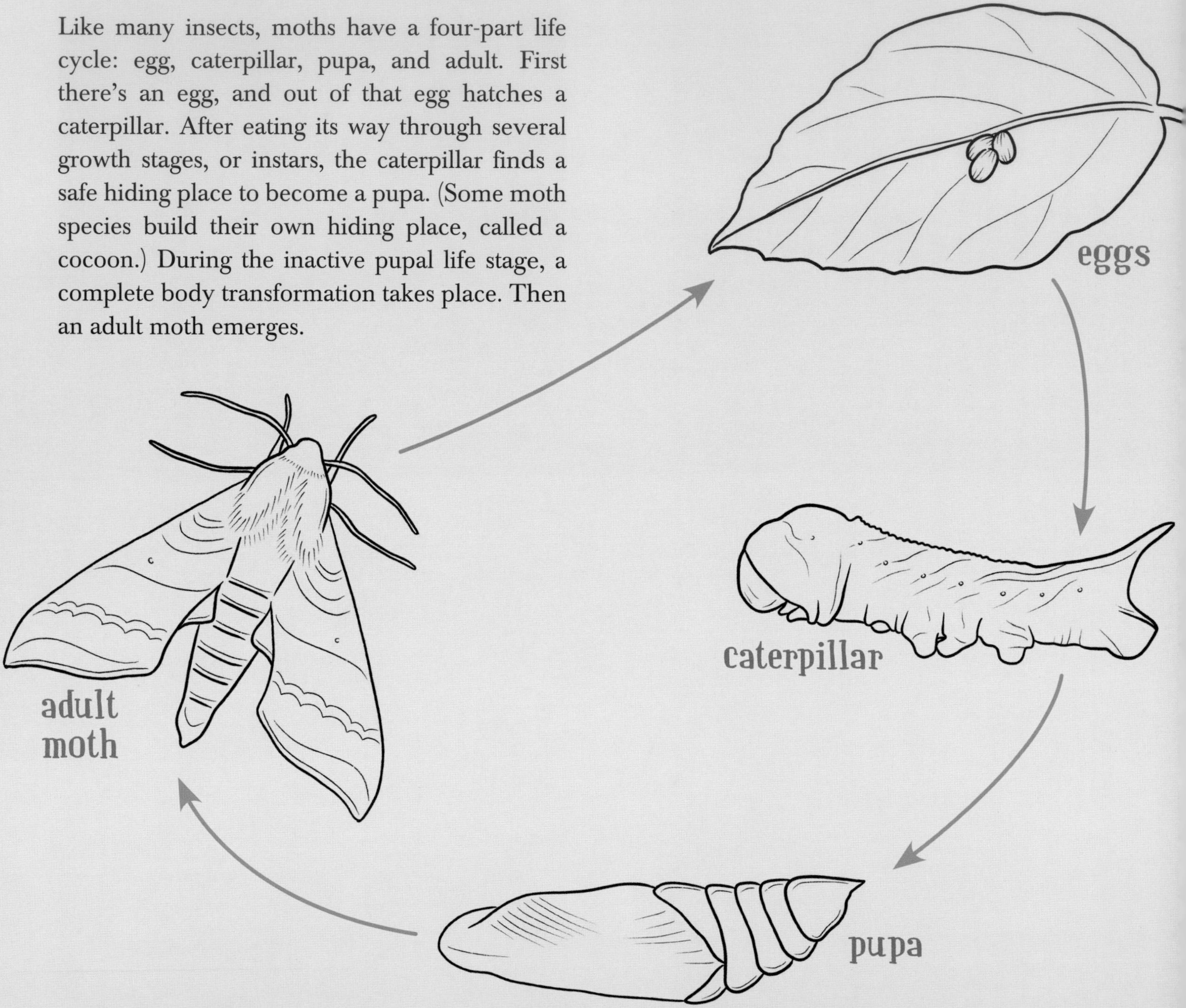

eggs

caterpillar

pupa

adult
moth

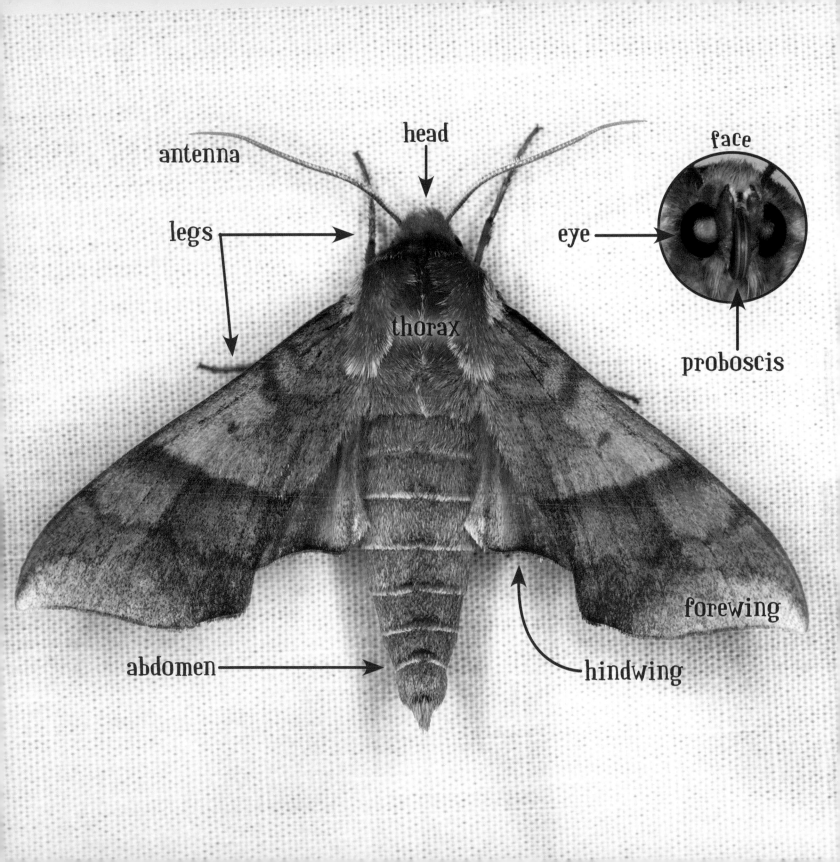

antenna

head

face

legs

eye

thorax

proboscis

abdomen

hindwing

forewing

MOTH BALL SUPPLIES AND SETUP

Be sure to invite some grown-ups to your moth ball to help. Important note: Never look directly into any light. That can harm your eyes. Look at the moths instead! You can also purchase special glasses to protect your eyes from ultraviolet light.

The moth-watching tools shown in this book include a notebook and pencil, a camera, a loupe and a magnifying glass (for looking at moths up close), a flashlight, a headlamp, and a ruler. The moth-attracting supplies include a rope, a sheet, and some clothespins, as well as an extension cord and various types of black light.

The type of light you choose will affect the number and variety of moths you attract. Blacklight bulbs are easy to locate (most hardware stores carry them) but aren't strong enough to attract a lot of moths. (If you go this route, get the CFL type, not the incandescent.) A better option is an ultraviolet light marketed for attracting moths. Online vendors that sell supplies for studying insects carry them. The most useful light for inviting moths, in our experience, is a mercury vapor bulb, which you can purchase at your local pet store. (Reptile owners use them to keep their pets cozy!) Different moth species are attracted to different types of light. The more light sources you have, the more moth visitors you can expect. Whichever light you choose, be sure to follow the safety instructions provided.

There are endless options for setting up a lighting station. For the moth ball events shown in this book, we hung a rope between two trees, pinned a white sheet to it, and then shone our light onto the sheet. You could also hang a sheet from the side of a house or garage, or even pin a pillowcase to a porch wall. In fact, a sheet isn't even necessary. Moths will come to lights regardless of whether there is a sheet for them to perch on.

One last note: You might also want insect repellent. Especially in the first hours after sundown, mosquitoes can be plentiful. The good news is that they usually taper off as the night goes on.

Baiting and Bait Recipe

Invite your favorite adult to help make your moth bait. The ingredients include raw fruit, sugar, and a splash of alcohol. (The kind people drink, not the kind from the pharmacy.) You'll find hundreds of recipes online. The secret to a great bait, we've learned, is letting the mixture rot a bit before serving. Our bait included three very brown bananas (fresh or frozen), half a cup of brown sugar, half a cup of stale beer, and a splash of rum. This concoction was thick and goopy and, after a week on the kitchen counter, seriously smelly. The moths loved it.

Bait is typically painted onto tree trunks, but we found that fence posts work just as well!

ONE LAST THING

We consulted several entomologists (insect scientists), and they all agreed that using lights is not harmful to your local moth population. Neither is leaving the lights on overnight. If you do this, however, be sure to get up early to see which moths have stopped by, and then shake your sheet to send them on their way. Otherwise, as the sun rises, birds will swoop in and eat your moths for breakfast!

AUTHOR'S NOTE

Whenever I want to explore something new, be it how to make a quilt or how to grow potatoes or how to study moths, my first step is always the same: I look for a mentor. A mentor is someone who has mastered the skill you are looking to acquire and who is willing to guide you. When I needed help identifying the moths in my backyard, a friend introduced me to Teá Kesting-Handly, who has been studying moths for years.

Teá taught me a lot. One night, at a moth ball in my yard, she caught a luna moth. "This one is a female," she said, handing the gorgeous moth to me, "and its wings are very worn."

I didn't understand why this was important, but Teá told me in an excited voice, "Adult lunas only live for about a week. Females mate quickly and begin laying eggs right away. Because this moth has wings that are worn, I know she's on the older side and so has probably already mated."

I still wasn't sure why this was exciting, so Teá made it clear: "You could take this moth inside and gently place her in a paper bag and leave the closed bag on a counter overnight. In the morning, let the luna go. If you're lucky, she'll have left you some eggs inside the bag."

I followed Teá's suggestions. And in the morning, just as my mentor had predicted, there were a dozen eggs inside that brown bag. Luna moth eggs! In my very own kitchen! Those eggs were the start of an entirely new moth adventure—raising them—but that is a story for another book.

I hope you study the moths where you live. And I hope you'll find a moth enthusiast who can help you. Good places to look for a mentor include your family (is your great-aunt an entomologist or is your third cousin into beetles?), your school (check with your science teacher or the nature club), and your nearest nature center.

Happy mothing!

Loree   Ellen's shadow

PHOTOGRAPHER'S NOTE

Making photos outside at night is very hard. Even the best cameras can "see" only a fraction of the shades of gray and colors that our eyes can see at night. Illuminating scenes so they are bright enough to see the subjects but still dark enough to capture the experience was a delicate balance.

Photographing the moths close up was simple once I figured out my camera settings. Once moths land on the white sheet, they tend to stay fairly still. Shooting in manual mode with a macro lens, I closed down my aperture (the lens opening) to give me the greatest depth of field (f16–22). I placed my shutter speed between 1/100 and 1/200, and I set my ISO at 200. I used a ring light for most of the moth shots, with an occasional boost from a flashlight or cell phone. People at the moth balls also captured great images with cell phones with the help of a headlamp or flashlight.

The hard part was photographing moth ball scenes from a distance. A tripod was required to stabilize my camera while using a very slow shutter speed, a narrow depth of field, a high ISO, and no on-camera flash. I needed other light sources to help illuminate the scene. I used the lights in front of and behind the sheet. The ultraviolet fluorescent tube cast a blue light, while the mercury vapor lamp provided a bright white light that created great shadows. For other images, I used a headlamp or a lantern.

One night in July, Loree and I were practicing for an upcoming moth ball. While we were waiting for the moths, the mosquitoes came out in force. It was so unbearable that Loree and I put on hooded beekeeper jackets to protect our arms and faces. We decided to have some fun while waiting for the moths and started playing with light painting. To make photos painted with light, I placed my camera on a tripod and used a very slow shutter speed (twenty seconds). Loree set her headlamp on red mode and made a giant heart shape. She then quickly switched the lamp to the white light and made an arrow through the heart.

Light played a very significant role in this book, just as much as the moths and the people who came to see them.

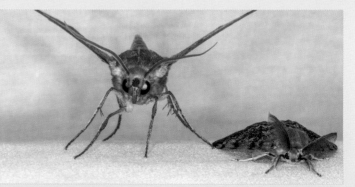

GLOSSARY

Abdomen: rearmost part of a moth's body

Antennae: pair of sensory organs on a moth's head

Bait: sugary liquid used to attract moths

Cocoon: silk covering in which some caterpillars spend their pupal life stage

Forewings: set of wings closest to the moth's head

Habitat: natural environment in which an organism makes its home

Hindwings: set of wings closest to the moth's abdomen

Insect: small creature with an exoskeleton, six legs, and sometimes wings

Nectar: sugary liquid produced by many plants

Proboscis: tubelike mouthpart of an adult moth

Thorax: part of the moth's body to which its legs and wings are attached

RESOURCES

Further Reading

Arnosky, Jim. *Crinkleroot's Guide to Knowing Butterflies and Moths*. New York: Simon & Schuster, 1996.

Opler, Paul A. *Peterson First Guide to Butterflies and Moths*. Boston: Houghton Mifflin, 1994.

Bibliography

Beadle, David, and Seabrooke Leckie. *Peterson Field Guide to Moths of Northeastern North America*. Boston: Houghton Mifflin Harcourt, 2012.

Himmelman, John. *Discovering Moths: Nighttime Jewels in Your Own Backyard*. Camden, ME: Down East Books, 2002.

Websites

BugGuide
www.bugguide.net

Butterflies and Moths of North America
www.butterfliesandmoths.org

Discover Life
www.discoverlife.org/moth

The Lepidopterists' Society
www.lepsoc.org

National Moth Week
www.nationalmothweek.org

North America Moth Photographers Group
www.mothphotographersgroup.msstate.edu

To see more images of moths that Ellen created during the making of this book, visit http://tinyurl.com/MothBallPhotos.